A

General Works

Library of Congress Classification
2012

Prepared by the Policy and Standards Division
Library Services

LIBRARY OF CONGRESS
Cataloging Distribution Service
Washington, D.C.

LIBRARY OF CONGRESS

This edition cumulates all additions and changes to class A through List 2012/08, dated August 20, 2012. Additions and changes made subsequent to that date are published in lists posted on the World Wide Web at

<http://www.loc.gov/aba/cataloging/classification/weeklylists/>

and are also available in *Classification Web*, the online Web-based edition of the Library of Congress Classification.

Library of Congress Cataloging-in-Publication Data

Library of Congress.
   Library of Congress classification. A. General works / prepared by the Policy
and Standards Division, Library Services. — 2012 edition.
       pages cm
   "This edition cumulates all additions and changes to class A through List 2012/08,
dated August 20, 2012. Additions and changes made subsequent to that date are published in
lists posted on the World Wide Web ... and are also available in *Classification Web*,
the online Web-based edition of the Library of Congress classification." -- Title page verso."
   Includes index.
   ISBN 978-0-8444-9557-6
   1. Classification, Library of Congress. 2. Classification—Books—General works. I. Library
of Congress. Policy and Standards Division. II. Title. III. Title: General works.
   Z696.U5A 2012
   025.4'33—dc22

                              2012037585

For sale by the Library of Congress Cataloging Distribution Service,
101 Independence Avenue, S.E., Washington, DC 20541-4912.
Product catalog available on the Web at **www.loc.gov/cds**.

PREFACE

The first edition of Class A, General Works, was published in 1911, the second in 1915, the third in 1947 (reprinted in 1953), and the fourth in 1973. A 1998 edition cumulated additions and changes that were made during the period 1973-1998, and was followed by the 2008 edition. This 2012 edition cumulates additions and changes made since the publication of the 2008 edition.

In the Library of Congress Classification schedules, classification numbers or spans of numbers that appear in parentheses are formerly valid numbers that are now obsolete. Numbers or spans that appear in angle brackets are optional numbers that have never been used at the Library of Congress but are provided for other libraries that wish to use them. In most cases, a parenthesized or angle-bracketed number is accompanied by a "see" reference directing the user to the actual number that the Library of Congress currently uses, or a note explaining Library of Congress practice.

Access to the online version of the full Library of Congress Classification is available on the World Wide Web by subscription to Classification Web. Details about ordering and pricing may be obtained from the Cataloging Distribution Service at:

<http://www.loc.gov/cds/>

New or revised numbers and captions are added to the L.C. Classification schedules as a result of development proposals made by the cataloging staff of the Library of Congress and cooperating institutions. Upon approval of these proposals by the editorial meeting of the Policy and Standards Division, new classification records are created or existing records are revised in the master classification database. Lists of newly approved or revised classification numbers and captions are posted on the World Wide Web at:

<http://www.loc.gov/aba/cataloging/classification/weeklylists/>

Libby Dechman, senior subject cataloging policy specialist in the Policy and Standards Division, is responsible for coordinating the overall intellectual and editorial content of class A. Kent Griffiths and Ethel Tillman, assistant editors of classification schedules, are responsible for creating new classification records, maintaining the master database, and creating index terms for the captions.

Barbara B. Tillett, Chief
Policy and Standards Division

September 2012

OUTLINE

TABLES

INDEX

Collections. Series. Collected works
Collections of monographs, essays, etc.
Prefer subclass AS for collections published under the auspices
of learned bodies (Institutions or societies)
Prefer class D for collections mainly historical
Prefer class P for collections like Biblioteca de autores españoles,
Bibliotheca romanica, etc.
Translations are classed with the original language where
possible
American and English
1	Comprehensive collections
	Minor collections
	Including popular and juvenile collections, home study, "Festschriften" of general character, etc.
4	Early works through 1850
5	1851-
	Collected works of individual authors
6	16th and 17th centuries
7	18th century
8	19th and 20th centuries
	Other languages
9	General collections
(10)	Ancient languages
	see subclasses P-PM
	Medieval languages
	Class here collections that include both medieval and modern languages
11	Several authors (Two or more languages)
12	Individual authors
	Medieval and modern latin
13	Several authors
14	Individual authors
	Modern languages
15	Several authors (Two or more languages)
15.5	Individual authors
	European languages
	Dutch
	For Afrikaans see AC177+
16	Several authors
	Individual authors
17	16th and 17th centuries
18	18th century
19	19th-21st centuries
	French
20	Several authors
	Individual authors
21	16th and 17th centuries

	Collections of monographs, essays, etc.
	Other languages
	Modern languages
	European languages
	French
	Individual authors -- Continued
23	18th century
25	19th-21st centuries
	German
30	Several authors
	Individual authors
31	16th and 17th centuries
33	18th century
35	19th-21st centuries
	Italian
40	Several authors
	Individual authors
41	16th and 17th centuries
43	18th century
45	19th-21st centuries
	Scandinavian
50	Several authors
	Individual authors
51	16th and 17th centuries
53	18th century
55	19th-21st centuries
	Slavic
60	Several authors
	Individual authors
61	16th and 17th centuries
63	18th century
65	19th-21st centuries
	Spanish and Portuguese
70	Several authors
	Individual authors
71	16th and 17th centuries
73	18th century
75	19th-21st centuries
	Finnish and Estonian
80	Several authors
	Individual authors
81	16th and 17th centuries
83	18th century
85	19th-21st centuries
95.A-Z	Other European languages, A-Z
95.A4	Albanian
95.B3	Basque

Collections of monographs, essays, etc.
    Other languages
        Modern languages
            European languages
                Other European languages, A-Z -- Continued

95.B74	Breton
95.C3	Catalan
95.G8	Greek (Modern)
95.H9	Hungarian
95.I73	Irish
95.L36	Latvian
95.L5	Lithuanian
95.R8	Romanian
95.R82	Romansch
95.W44	Welsh

            Asian languages
                Semitic

101-102	Hebrew (Table A13)
103-104	Yiddish (Table A13)
105-106	Arabic (Table A13)

                Indo-Aryan

111-112	Classical and medieval (Table A13)

                    Modern

117-118	Bengali (Table A13)
119-120	Gujarati (Table A13)
121-122	Hindi (Table A13)
125.A-Z	Other Indic, A-Z
	Assamese
125.A7	Several authors
125.A72	Individual authors
	Bhojpuri
125.B46	Several authors
125.B462	Individual authors
	Dogri
125.D629	Several authors
125.D73	Individual authors
	Maithili
125.M25	Several authors
125.M252	Individual authors
	Marathi
125.M3	Several authors
125.M32	Individual authors
	Nepali
125.N37	Several authors
125.N372	Individual authors
	Oriya
125.O7	Several authors

	Collections of monographs, essays, etc.
	Other languages
	Modern languages
	Austronesian languages
	Other, A-Z
	Javanese -- Continued
176.J392	Individual authors
	African languages
177-178	Afrikaans (Table A13)
179-180	Bantu (Table A13)
189.A-Z	Other, A-Z
189.A45	Amharic
189.M34	Malagasy
189.S9	Swahili
190.A-Z	Hyperborean languages, A-Z
195.A-Z	American Indian languages, A-Z
200	Collections for Jewish readers
	Inaugural and program dissertations
	Prefer classification by subject in Classes B-Z
801	American (United States)
811	English
817	Dutch
819	Finnish
821	French
825	Belgian
831	German and Austrian
835	Hungarian
841	Italian
	Scandinavian
851	Collective
852	Danish
853	Icelandic
854	Norwegian
855	Swedish
	Slavic
861	Russian
865	Polish
869.A-Z	Other Slavic, A-Z
871	Spanish and Portuguese
875	Swiss
895.A-Z	Other, A-Z
	Pamphlet collections
901	American and English
911	English (exclusively)
917	Dutch
921	French
931	German

	Pamphlet collections -- Continued
941	Italian
951	Scandinavian
961	Slavic
971	Spanish and Portuguese
995.A-Z	Other, A-Z
999	Scrapbooks
1100	Electronic media collections

	Encyclopedias
	Translations class with the new language, not the original work
1	History, method of use, etc.
1.5	Authorship. Handbooks for compilers
	Encyclopedic works
	Early works
2	To end of middle ages (1450/1515)
3	End of middle ages through 16th century
4	17th and 18th centuries
	Prefer AE5+ for works in alphabetic form
	Modern encyclopedias. By language
	American and English
5	General
6	Encyclopedic works in other than alphabetic form
	American (United States and Canada) in languages other than English or Spanish
7	French-American
8	German-American
9	Italian-American
10.A-Z	Other, A-Z
10.3	Afrikaans
10.4	Albanian
10.55	Arabic
10.6	Armenian
10.65	Assamese
(11)	Austrian
	see AE27
11.3	Azerbaijani
14	Basque
15	Belgian
15.3	Bengali
15.7	Burmese
16	Catalan
17	Chinese
19	Dutch
20	Estonian
21	Finnish
25	French
25.5	Galician
26	Georgian
27	German
29	Greek (Modern)
29.5	Gujarati
30	Hebrew
30.5	Hindi
31	Hungarian
33	Indonesian

	Encyclopedic works
	Modern encyclopedias. By language -- Continued
35	Italian
35.2	Japanese
35.23	Javanese
35.3	Kannada
35.37	Kazakh
35.38	Kirghiz
35.4	Korean
35.45	Kurdish
35.5	Latvian
35.55	Lithuanian
35.6	Malagasy
35.615	Malay
35.62	Malayalam
35.67	Marathi
35.78	Moldavian
35.79	Mongolian
35.83	Nepali
35.88	Oriya
35.9	Panjabi
36	Persian
37	Portuguese
39	Romanian
	Scandinavian
41	Danish
42	Icelandic
43	Norwegian
45	Swedish
48	Sindhi
49	Sinhalese
	Slavic
51	Czech
53	Polish
55	Russian
59	Serbian. Croatian
60.A-Z	Other Slavic, A-Z
	e.g.
60.B8	Bulgarian
60.S58	Slovak
60.U4	Ukrainian
60.W47	White Russian
	Spanish
61	General
65	Spanish-American
(69)	Swiss
	see AE25, AE27, or AE35

Encyclopedic works
  Modern encyclopedias. By language -- Continued
69.7   Tajik
70   Tamil
70.3   Tatar
70.6   Telugu
71   Thai
73   Tibetan
75   Turkish
75.3   Turkmen
76.5   Urdu
77   Uzbek
78   Vietnamese
80   Welsh
88   Yiddish
(90)   Other
                see AE5+
  Electronic encyclopedias. Online encyclopedias
      Including encyclopedias with user-generated content
      Class electronic and online versions of printed encyclopedias
          with the print version
      For general works on user-generated content see
          ZA4482
91   General works
100   Wikipedia

Dictionaries and other general reference works
Class translations with the language of the translation rather than
with the language of the original text
2 General collections of reference works
Including electronic reference sources
Dictionaries. Minor encyclopedias
Including popular and juvenile works
4 International. Polyglot
Other
American and English
5 General
6 Encyclopedic works in other than alphabetic form
American (United States and Canada) in languages other
than English or Spanish
7 French-American
8 German-American
9 Italian-American
10.A-Z Other, A-Z
10.3 Afrikaans
10.4 Albanian
10.55 Arabic
10.6 Armenian
10.65 Assamese
(11) Austrian
see AG27
11.3 Azerbaijani
14 Basque
15 Belgian
15.3 Bengali
15.7 Burmese
16 Catalan
17 Chinese
19 Dutch
20 Estonian
21 Finnish
25 French
26 Georgian
27 German
29 Greek (Modern)
29.5 Gujarati
30 Hebrew
30.5 Hindi
31 Hungarian
33 Indonesian
35 Italian
35.2 Japanese

Dictionaries. Minor encyclopedias
Other -- Continued

35.3	Kannada
35.37	Kazakh
35.38	Kirghiz
35.4	Korean
35.44	Kurdish
35.5	Latvian
35.55	Lithuanian
35.6	Malagasy
35.62	Malayalam
35.67	Marathi
35.78	Moldovan
35.783	Mongolian
35.83	Nepali
35.88	Oriya
35.9	Panjabi
36	Persian
37	Portuguese
39	Romanian
	Scandinavian
41	Danish
43	Norwegian
45	Swedish
49	Sinhalese
	Slavic
51	Czech
53	Polish
55	Russian
59	Serbian. Croatian
60.A-Z	Other Slavic, A-Z
	e.g.
60.B8	Bulgarian
60.S58	Slovak
60.U4	Ukrainian
60.W47	White Russian. Belarusian
	Spanish
61	General
65	Spanish-American
(69)	Swiss
	see AG25, AG27, or AG35
69.7	Tajik
70	Tamil
70.6	Telugu
71	Thai
73	Tibetan

	Dictionaries. Minor encyclopedias
	Other -- Continued
75	Turkish
75.3	Turkmen
76.5	Urdu
77	Uzbek
78	Vietnamese
80	Welsh
88	Yiddish
(90)	Other
	see AG5+
	General works, pocketbooks, receipts, etc.
103	Early works through 1600
104	17th and 18th centuries
	Later
	American and English
105	General works
106	Encyclopedic works in other than alphabetic form
	American (United States and Canada) in languages other than English or Spanish
107	French-American
108	German-American
109	Italian-American
110.A-Z	Other, A-Z
110.3	Afrikaans
110.4	Albanian
110.55	Arabic
110.6	Armenian
110.65	Assamese
(111)	Austrian
	see AG127
111.3	Azerbaijani
114	Basque
115	Belgian
115.3	Bengali
115.7	Burmese
116	Catalan
117	Chinese
119	Dutch
120	Estonian
121	Finnish
125	French
126	Georgian
127	German
129	Greek (Modern)
129.5	Gujarati

General works, pocketbooks, receipts, etc.
Later -- Continued

130	Hebrew
130.5	Hindi
131	Hungarian
133	Indonesian
135	Italian
135.2	Japanese
135.3	Kannada
135.37	Kazakh
135.38	Kirghiz
135.4	Korean
135.5	Latvian
135.55	Lithuanian
135.6	Malagasy
135.62	Malayalam
135.67	Marathi
135.78	Moldavian
135.83	Nepali
135.88	Oriya
135.9	Panjabi
136	Persian
137	Portuguese
139	Romanian
	Scandinavian
141	Danish
143	Norwegian
145	Swedish
	Slavic
151	Czech
153	Polish
155	Russian
159	Serbian. Croatian
160.A-Z	Other Slavic, A-Z
	e.g.
160.B8	Bulgarian
160.S58	Slovak
160.U4	Ukrainian
160.W47	White Russian
	Spanish
161	General
165	Spanish-American
(169)	Swiss
	see AG125, AG127, or AG135
169.7	Tajik
170	Tamil

	General works, pocketbooks, receipts, etc.
	Later -- Continued
170.6	Telugu
171	Thai
175	Turkish
175.3	Turkmen
176.5	Urdu
177	Uzbek
180	Welsh
188	Yiddish
(190)	Other
	see AG105+
	Questions and answers
	Cf. GV1507.Q5 Quiz books
195	American and English
196.A-Z	Other languages, A-Z
	e.g.
196.F8	French
196.G3	German
196.S6	Spanish
	Reference books for special classes of persons
(211)	Children
	see AG5+
(221)	Women
	see AG5+
	Wonders. Curiosities. Eccentric characters, fads, etc.
240	Periodicals
241	Early works through 1850/1870
243	1871-
250	Pictorial works (Views, events, etc.)
	Cf. G136+ Geography
	Notes and queries
	For notes and queries concerning bibliographical
	information see Z1034
305	American and English
307	Dutch
309	French
313	Italian
	Clipping bureaus
500	Periodicals
501	Associations
511	General works
513	Organization. Methods
519	Miscellaneous
	By region or country
	United States

	Clipping bureaus. Information bureaus
	By region or country
	United States -- Continued
521	General works
527.A-Z	Special institutions. By place, A-Z
531.A-Z	Other American regions or countries, A-Z
541.A-Z	European regions or countries, A-Z
551.A-Z	Other regions or countries, A-Z
(571)	Information dissemination by traveling educational exhibit -- show cars, movies, etc.
	see LC6691
600	Free material. Lists of free material not limited to a special subject
	Cf. Z5817.2 Bibliography of teaching aids

Indexes
    Class here only general indexes
    Class indexes to particular works with the work, except for indexes
       to particular newspapers which class in AI21
    For indexes limited to special subjects, see class Z
    For works on the technique of indexing as well as works on
       the use, value, etc., of indexes see Z695.9+

1	Periodicals. Societies
	By language of index
3	English
5	Dutch
7	French
9	German
11	Italian
13	Scandinavian
15	Slavic
	For Balto-Slavic languages see AI19.A+
17	Spanish and Portuguese
19.A-Z	Other, A-Z
19.A47	Afrikaans
19.A52	Albanian
19.A6	Arabic
19.A7	Armenian
19.B3	Baluchi
19.B46	Bengali
19.B85	Burmese
19.C5	Chinese
19.E77	Estonian
19.F5	Finnish
19.G4	Georgian
19.G73	Greek, Modern
19.G85	Gujarati
19.H8	Hungarian
19.I5	Indic
19.I55	Indonesian
19.J3	Japanese
19.J33	Javanese
19.K34	Kannada
19.K39	Kazakh
19.K6	Korean
19.L3	Latin
19.L34	Latvian
19.L5	Lithuanian
19.M32	Malay
19.M34	Malayalam
19.N46	Nepali
19.R6	Romanian

Museums. Collectors and collecting
　　Class here general works only
　　For museums and collections in special fields, see classes B-Z
1　　Periodicals. Societies. Collections, etc.
　　　　Class here publications devoted to the interests of museums,
　　　　　　methodology, description, etc.
　　　　For serials or collections of scientific contributions, memoirs, etc.,
　　　　　　see AC, AS, and B-Z
2　　Congresses
3　　Dictionaries. Encyclopedias
　　Biography
3.5　　Collective
3.6.A-Z　　Individual, A-Z
　　General works
4　　Early works through 1800
5　　1801-
7　　General special
　　　　Includes educational aspects, relations, etc.
8　　Children's museums
　　　　Class here general works only
　　　　For museums of special countries see AM10+
　　　　For individual children's museums see AM101.A+
9　　Minor. Pamphlets, etc.
　　Description and history of museums
　　　By region or country
　　　　For individual museums of a general nature see
　　　　　AM101.A+
　　　America
10　　　General works
11-13　　　United States (Table A14)
21-22　　　British America. Canada (Table A15)
23-24　　　Mexico (Table A15)
　　　　Central America
25　　　　General works
26.A-Z　　　　By region or country, A-Z
　　　　　Subarrange individual countries by Table A17
　　　　West Indies
29　　　　General works
30.A-Z　　　　By region or country, A-Z
　　　　　Subarrange individual countries by Table A17
　　　　South America
33　　　　General works
34.A-Z　　　　By region or country, A-Z
　　　　　Subarrange individual countries by Table A17
　　　Europe
40　　　General works
　　　Great Britain

Description and history of museums
By region or country
Europe
Great Britain -- Continued

41	General works
42.A-Z	Constituent countries, counties, etc., A-Z
	Subarrange individual countries by Table A17
	e.g.
42.I7-.I73	Ireland. Éire (Table A17)
42.N6-.N63	Northern Ireland (Table A17)
43.A-Z	Cities, towns, etc., A-Z
44-45	Austria (Table A15)
45.2	Czechoslovakia. Czech Republic (Table A16)
45.3	Slovakia (Table A16)
45.5	Hungary (Table A16)
46-48	France (Table A14)
49-51	Germany (Table A14)
	Including West Germany
51.5	East Germany (Table A16)
52-53	Greece (Table A15)
54-55	Italy (Table A15)
	Netherlands
56	Belgium (Table A16)
57-59	Holland (Table A14)
	Russia
60.A1	Periodicals. Societies
60.A2	General works
60.A3-Z	Regions, provinces, etc., A-Z
	Subarrange individual countries by Table A17
	e.g.
60.C4	Central Asia
60.C5	Chelyabinsk (Province)
(60.E8)	Estonia
	see AM70.E75
(60.L3)	Latvia
	see AM70.L3
(60.L5)	Lithuania
	see AM70.L5
60.M6	Moscow (Province)
(60.U4)	Ukraine
	see AM70.U38
60.U9-.U93	Uzbekistan (Table A17)
61.A-Z	Cities, towns, etc., A-Z
	Scandinavia
61.5	General works
62	Denmark (Table A16)
63	Norway (Table A16)

AM

	Description and history of museums
	By region or country
	Arab countries -- Continued
79.5.A-Z	Individual Arab countries, A-Z
	Subarrange individual countries by Table A17
	For individual North African countries see AM91.A+
79.5.B26-.B263	Bahrain (Table A17)
	Egypt see AM87+
	Africa
80	General works
87-88	Egypt (Table A15)
89-90	South Africa (Table A15)
91.A-Z	Other African countries, A-Z
	Subarrange individual countries by Table A17
	e.g.
91.M3-.M33	Malawi (Table A17)
91.M69-.M693	Mozambique (Table A17)
91.N6-.N63	Nigeria (Table A17)
93-95	Australia (Table A14)
96-98	New Zealand (Table A14)
99-100	Pacific islands (Table A15)
101.A-Z	Individual museums. By place, A-Z
	Some older and larger museums have been subarranged by Table A1 in the Library of Congress shelflist. For numbers already so treated, continue to apply Table A1
	Museology. Museum methods, technique, etc.
111	General works
	Prefer AM5
121	Organization. Management
122	Finance
(123)	Architecture
	see NA6700
124	Public relations
125	Communication of museum information
	Equipment
127	General works
129	Furniture
130	Cleaning
	The collections
133	General works
135	Collecting
	Cf. QH61+ Natural history
139	Registration. Accessioning
	Preparation and preservation
141	General works
145	Special methods (not A-Z)

	Museology. Museum methods, technique, etc.
	The collections
	Preparation and preservation -- Continued
	Special subjects
	see the caption "Museums" in Classes B-Z
148	Security measures
	Exhibition
	Cf. T391+ Technological exhibitions
151	General works
153	Classification. Arrangement
157	Labels. Marketing
158	Archives
	Service to special groups
160	People with disabilities
	Collectors and collecting. Collectibles. Private collections
	Class here general works only
	For special subjects see classes B-Z
	Periodicals, societies, etc.
200	International
201	English
203	French
205	German
207.A-Z	Other, A-Z
211	Dictionaries
213	Directories
215	Computer network resources
	Including the Internet
221	History of collecting
223	Biography of collectors (Collective)
	For individual biographies see AM401.A+
231	General works
235	Addresses, essays, lectures
236	Catalogs of collectibles
237	Collectibles as an investment
	For specific collectible items, see the item, e.g. HE6184.I5,
	Postage stamps
	By region or country
301	America
302	North America
	United States
303	General works
303.5	Catalogs of collectibles
304	Colonial period
305	19th-20th centuries
306	New England
307	South
308	West

Collectors and collecting. Collectibles. Private collections
By region or country
United States -- Continued
310.A-.W   States, A-W
311.A-Z   Cities, A-Z
313   Canada
314   Mexico
Central America
315   General works
316   Belize
317   Costa Rica
318   Guatemala
319   Honduras
320   Nicaragua
321   El Salvador
322   Panama
West Indies
323   General works
324   Bahamas
325   Cuba
326   Haiti
327   Jamaica
328   Puerto Rico
329.A-Z   Other, A-Z
South America
330   General works
331   Argentina
332   Bolivia
333   Brazil
334   Chile
335   Colombia
336   Ecuador
337   Guiana
338   Paraguay
339   Peru
340   Uruguay
341   Venezuela
Europe
342   General works
Great Britain. England
343   General works
344   England -- Local
345   Scotland
346   Ireland
347   Wales
348   Austria
348.2   Czechoslovakia. Czech Republic

Collectors and collecting. Collectibles. Private collections
By region or country
Europe -- Continued

348.3	Slovakia
348.5	Finland
349	France
350	Germany
351	Greece
351.5	Hungary
352	Italy
	Netherlands
353	General works
354	Belgium
355	Holland
355.5	Poland
356	Russia
	Scandinavia
357	General works
358	Denmark
359	Iceland
360	Norway
361	Sweden
362	Spain
363	Portugal
364	Switzerland
	Turkey and other Balkan states
365	General works
366	Turkey
367	Bulgaria
368	Albania
369	Romania
370	Yugoslavia
371.A-Z	Other, A-Z
	Asia. The Orient
372	General works
	Southwestern Asia
373	General. Levant. Turkey in Asia
374	Iran
374.5	Iraq
375	Israel
	Southern Asia
376	General. India. Pakistan. Ceylon
377	Vietnam
378	Thailand
379	Malaysia
380	Indonesia
381	Philippines

Newspapers

A classification schedule for newspapers has not been developed

Domestic newspapers at the Library of Congress are arranged in checklists and on shelves as follows: [1] By state; [2] By city, town, etc.; [3] By important word in title. Eighteenth century newspapers are arranged by first word of title (excluding the initial article of the title); [4] By date

Foreign newspapers at the Library of Congress are arranged in checklists and on the shelves as follows: [1] By country; [2] By city, town, etc.; [3] By first word in title (excluding the initial article of the title); [4] By date

For history and description of individual newspapers, see PN4899+

Periodicals
>Class periodicals by language; under languages periodicals are
grouped geographically
>Class here only periodicals of a general nature not limited to a
specific subject
>For periodicals devoted to a special subject, see the subject in
classes B - Z, e. g. PR1, English literature; PS1, American
literature; etc.
>Class selections from periodicals in AC or with the subject in
classes A- Z
>For publications of learned societies see AS1+
>For history of periodicals (classified in Subclass AP) see
PN4699+

1	International polyglot
	e.g.
1.C8	Cosmopolis
	English
	United States
2.A2	Through 1800
	Including early 19th century periodicals whose publication ceased before 1820
2.A3-.Z7	1801-
2.Z8	Periodicals with only one issue
2.Z9	Curiosa
	Periodicals and magazines in foreign languages published in the United States
	see AP16, AP21, AP31, etc.
	For American editions of British periodicals see AP4
	Great Britain (and continental Europe)
3	Early through 1800
4	1801-
	Class here American editions of British periodicals
5	Canada
6	Western hemisphere (except the United States and Canada)
7	Australia
7.5	New Zealand
7.7	Pacific islands
8	Asia
9	Africa
	Dutch and Flemish
	Holland and Belgium
14	Early through 1800
15	1801-
16	America
17.A-Z	Other countries, A-Z
18	Afrikaans
	French

AP

	French -- Continued
20	France
	America
21.A2	Early through 1800
21.A3-Z	1801-
	Europe (except France)
22	Belgium
24	Switzerland
25	Other countries of Europe (not A-Z)
26	Asia
27	Africa
28	Australia
28.5	New Zealand
28.7	Pacific Islands
	German
30	Germany and Austria
31	America
32	Switzerland
33	Europe (except Germany, Austria, and Switzerland)
34	Asia
35	Africa
36	Australia
36.5	New Zealand
36.7	Pacific islands
	Italian
37	Italy
38	America
39	Other countries (not A-Z)
	Scandinavian
40	General
41	Icelandic
	Danish
42	Denmark and other countries (except America)
43	America
	Norwegian
45	Norway and other countries (except America)
46	America
	Swedish
48	Sweden and other countries (except America)
49	America
	Slavic
	Russian
	For languages in Russia, other than Russian, see AP4, AP25, AP33, etc.
50	Russia and other countries (except America)
51	America
	Czech

	Slavic
	Czech -- Continued
52	Czech Republic and other countries (except America)
53	America
	Polish
54	Poland and other countries (except America)
55	America
56	Serbian and Croatian
58.A-Z	Other. By language, A-Z
	e.g.
	Baltic (Latvian) see AP95.L4
	Baltic (Lithuanian) see AP95.L5
	Belarusian see AP58.W5
58.B8	Bulgarian
58.M25	Macedonian
58.S53	Slovak
58.S55	Slovenian
58.S6	Sorbian
58.U5	Ukrainian
	Wendic see AP58.S6
58.W5	White Russian. Belarusian
	Spanish
60	Spain
61	Philippines
	America
62	United States
63	Latin America
64	Other countries (not A-Z)
	Portuguese
65	Portugal
66	South America
67	United States
68	Other countries (not A-Z)
(68.2)	Swiss
	see AP24, AP32, AP39, or AP95.R3
	Celtic
73	Irish
75	Scottish
77	Welsh
80	Finnish
	Hungarian
82	Hungary and other countries (except America)
83	America
85	Greek, Modern
86	Romanian
	General periodicals for Jewish readers
91	Hebrew and Yiddish

General periodicals for Jewish readers -- Continued

92	English
93	Other languages
95.A-Z	Other periodicals. By language, A-Z
	e.g.:
95.A3	Albanian
95.A4	Amharic
95.A6	Arabic
	Armenian
95.A7	Armenia and other countries (except America)
95.A8	America
95.A85	Assamese
95.A92	Azerbaijani
95.B3	Baluchi
95.B4	Bengali
95.B55	Bisaya
95.B9	Burmese
95.C3	Catalan
	Chinese
95.C4	China and other countries (except America)
95.C5	America
95.C7	Congo
95.D6	Dogri
95.E37	Eskimo
95.E4	Estonian
95.F7	Frisian
95.G45	Georgian
95.G8	Gujarati
95.H2	Hawaiian
95.H5	Hindi
95.I46	Ilocano
95.I5	Indonesian
	Japanese
95.J2	Japan and other countries (except America)
95.J25	America
95.J3	Javanese
95.K3	Kannada
95.K33	Karelian
95.K35	Kazakh
95.K57	Konkani
95.K6	Korean
95.L35	Latin (Medieval and modern)
95.L4	Latvian
95.L5	Lithuanian
95.M2	Malagasy
95.M24	Malay
95.M25	Malayalam

	Other periodicals. By language, A-Z -- Continued
95.M3	Marathi
95.M84	Mundari
95.N4	Nepali
95.N43	Newari
95.O7	Oriya
95.P25	Panjabi
95.P3	Persian
95.P7	Provençal
95.R3	Raeto-Romance
95.R35	Rajasthani
95.R8	Rundi
95.S3	Sanskrit
95.S5	Sindhi
95.S54	Sinhalese
95.S6	Soyot
95.S8	Sundanese
95.S9	Swahili
95.T27	Tagalog
95.T28	Tajik
95.T3	Tamil
95.T34	Tatar
95.T4	Telugu
95.T8	Turkish
95.T83	Turkmen
95.U7	Urdu
	Vietnamese
95.V5	Vietnam and other countries (except America)
95.V55	America
	Humorous periodicals
	Class periodicals issued in more than one language with each language in which they are published
101.A-Z	American and English
	e.g.:
101.J8	Judge
101.L6	Life
101.P7	Puck
101.P8	Punch
103.A-Z	French
	e.g.:
103.C2	La Caricature
103.R4	Le Rire
105.A-Z	German
	e.g.:
105.F6	Fliegende blätter
105.F7	Der Floh
105.H8	Humoristische blätter

	Humorous periodicals
	German -- Continued
105.J8	Jugend
105.K6	Kladderadatsch
105.S5	Simplicissimus
107	Italian
109	Scandinavian
111	Spanish and Portuguese
115	Other
	Juvenile periodicals
200	Early through 1880
200.5	International. Polyglot
201.A-Z	American and English
	e.g.:
201.C18	Calling all girls
201.C535	Children's digest
201.H12	Harper's young people
201.J68	Junior scholastic
201.S3	St. Nicholas
201.Y8	Youth's companion
203	French
	German
205	General works
206	German-American (United States)
207	Italian
209	Scandinavian
211	Spanish and Portuguese
215.A-Z	Other. By language, A-Z
	Juvenile periodicals for Jewish readers
221	Hebrew and Yiddish
222	English
223.A-Z	Other languages. By language, A-Z
230	Juvenile periodicals for Blacks
(250-265)	Periodicals for women
	see the subject, e.g. AP2+, General periodicals for women readers; HQ1101, Periodicals devoted to women's interests, feminism, etc.
	see the subject, e. g. JF847, JK1800, etc., Suffrage periodicals
	see the subject, e. g. subclass TX, Domestic economy; subclass TT, Fashion magazines, needlework, fancy work, etc.
(250)	Early
(251)	American and English
(253)	French
	German
(255)	General works
(256)	German-American
(257)	Italian

	Periodicals for women -- Continued
(259)	Scandinavian
(261)	Spanish and Portuguese
(265.A-Z)	Other. By language, A-Z
(270-271)	Periodicals for Blacks
	see AP2+, general periodicals for Black readers
(270)	American and English
(271.A-Z)	Other. By language, A-Z

	Academies and learned societies
	Class here associations and learned societies of a general character
	For societies devoted to the cultivation of a particular science, see that science
	For subarrangement of publications of individual societies, see Tables A2-A4
	For societies of various description devoted mainly to the promotion of social interests see HS1+
1	Periodicals devoted to the interests of learned societies in general
2	Serial directories. Serial handbooks
	Cf. AS5 Nonserial handbooks
	International associations, congresses, conferences, etc.
2.5	General works
4.A-Z	Individual associations, etc., A-Z
	e.g.
4.C3	Catholic International Scientific Congress (Congrès Scientifique International des Catholiques)
	United Nations Educational, Scientific and Cultural Organization (UNESCO)
	Official documents
4.U8A1-.U8A5	Serials
4.U8A6-.U8Z	Monographs. By title
4.U82A-.U82Z	Committees, etc. By name, A-Z
4.U825A-.U825Z	Reports of national delegations. By country, A-Z
4.U83A-.U83Z	Individual authors, A-Z
	Including official publications of preliminary conferences
4.Z9A-.Z9Z	Projects for intellectual cooperation. By author, A-Z
5	Historical and descriptive literature. Handbooks
	For serial handbooks see AS2
6	Organization of societies, conventions, congresses, calendars of congresses, etc.
	Including committees
	For management of and participation in meetings for business enterprises see HF5734.5
	For handbooks of parliamentary procedure see JF515
7	Anniversary planning
8	Directories and lists
	Cf. AS2 Serial directories
8.5	Computer network resources
	Including the Internet
9	International serial publications
	Including the collections of extracts from the transactions of several learned societies
	For nonserial collections see AC1+
	By region or country

AS

	By region or country -- Continued
	America
	General
11	Periodicals devoted to the interests of learned societies in general
(12)	Yearbooks
	see AS11
	International associations, congresses, conferences, etc.
12.5	General works
	Individual associations, etc.
14	General works
14.Z9A-.Z9Z	Projects for intellectual cooperation. By author, A-Z
15	Historical and descriptive literature. Handbooks
	For yearbooks see AS11
	For directories and lists issued periodically see AS18
16	Organization of societies, conventions, congresses, etc.
	Including committees
	For management of and participation in meetings for business enterprises see HF5734.5
	For handbooks of parliamentary procedure see JF515
17	Anniversary planning
18	Directories and lists
	Cf. AS11 Serial directories
19	International serial publications
	Including the collections of extracts from the transactions of several learned societies
	For nonserial collections see AC1+
	United States
22	General works
	History
25	General works
28.A-Z	By region or state, A-Z
29.A-Z	By city, A-Z
29.5	Directories and lists
30	Learned periodicals
	Individual societies and institutions
	For learned periodicals of a society or institution see AS30
32	Carnegie Institution of Washington
35	National Endowment for the Humanities
36.A-Z	Other individual societies and institutions. By city, A-Z
	Subarrange individual societies or institutions by Table A4
	British North America. Canada
	Cf. AS64 British Honduras
	Cf. AS73 Jamaica

	By region or country
	America
	British North America. Canada -- Continued
40	General works
41	Learned periodicals
42.A-Z	Individual societies and institutions, A-Z
	Subarrange individual societies or institutions by Table A4
	Latin America
60	General works, histories, etc.
63	Mexico (Table A19)
	Central America
64	Belize (Table A19)
65	Costa Rica (Table A19)
66	Guatemala (Table A19)
67	Honduras (Table A19)
68	Nicaragua (Table A19)
69	El Salvador (Table A19)
70	Panama (Table A19)
	West Indies
71	Cuba (Table A19)
72	Haiti (Table A19)
73	Jamaica (Table A19)
74	Puerto Rico (Table A19)
75	Dominican Republic (Table A19)
75.2	Virgin Islands of the United States (Table A19)
75.25	Barbados (Table A19)
	South America
77	General works
78	Argentina (Table A19)
79	Bolivia (Table A19)
80	Brazil (Table A19)
81	Chile (Table A19)
82	Colombia (Table A19)
83	Ecuador (Table A19)
84	Guyana (British Guiana) (Table A19)
85	Suriname (Dutch Guiana) (Table A19)
86	French Guiana (Table A19)
87	Paraguay (Table A19)
88	Peru (Table A19)
89	Uruguay (Table A19)
90	Venezuela (Table A19)
	Europe
	General
91	Periodicals devoted to the interests of learned societies in general
(92)	Yearbooks
	see AS91

AS

	By region or country
	Europe
	General -- Continued
	International associations, congresses, conferences, etc.
92.5	General works
	Individual associations, etc.
94	General works
94.Z9A-.Z9Z	Projects for intellectual cooperation. By author, A-Z
95	Historical and descriptive literature. Handbooks
	For yearbooks see AS91
	For directories and lists issued periodically see AS98
96	Organization of societies, conventions, congresses, etc.
	Including committees
97	Anniversary planning
98	Directories and lists
	Cf. AS91 Serial directories
99	International serial publications
	Including the collections of extracts from the transactions of several learned societies
	For nonserial collections see AC1+
111-122	Great Britain. Ireland (Table A18)
125	Austria (Table A19)
131-142	Czechoslovakia. Czech Republic (Table A18)
143	Slovakia (Table A19)
145	Finland (Table A19)
151-162	France (Table A18)
171-182	Germany (Table A18)
191-202	Greece (Table A18)
205	Hungary (Table A19)
211-222	Italy (Table A18)
225	Malta (Table A19)
	Belgium
240	General works
241	Learned periodicals
242.A-Z	Individual societies and institutions. By city, A-Z
	Subarrange individual societies or institutions by Table A4
	For learned periodicals of a society or institution see AS241
	Netherlands (Holland)
242.5	General works
243	Learned periodicals
244.A-Z	Individual societies and institutions. By city, A-Z
	Subarrange individual societies or institutions by Table A4
	For learned periodicals of a society of institution see AS243
248	Poland (Table A19)
251-262	Russia (Table A18)

AS

	By region or country
	Europe
	Spain -- Continued
302.A-Z	Individual societies and institutions. By city, A-Z
	Subarrange individual societies or institutions by Table A4
	For learned periodicals of a society or institution see AS301
	Portugal
302.5	General works
303	Learned periodicals
304.A-Z	Individual societies and institutions. By city, A-Z
	Subarrange individual societies or institutions by Table A4
	For learned periodicals of a society or institution see AS303
311-322	Switzerland (Table A18)
	Turkey and the Balkans
336	General works
342	Albania (Table A19)
342.5	Bosnia and Hercegovina (Table A19)
343	Bulgaria (Table A19)
	Montenegro see AS346
343.5	Croatia (Table A19)
343.7	Macedonia (Republic) (Table A19)
345	Romania (Table A19)
345.3	Serbia (Table A19)
345.5	Slovenia (Table A19)
346	Yugoslavia (Table A19)
348	Turkey (Table A19)
	Asia
	General
401	Periodicals devoted to the interests of learned societies in general
(402)	Yearbooks
	see AS401
	International associations, congresses, conferences, etc.
402.5	General works
	Individual associations, etc.
404	General works
404.Z9A-.Z9Z	Projects for intellectual cooperation. By author, A-Z
405	Historical and descriptive literature. Handbooks
	For yearbooks see AS401
	For directories and lists issued periodically see AS408
406	Organization of societies, conventions, congresses, etc.
	Including committees
407	Anniversary planning

	By region or country
	Asia
	General -- Continued
408	Directories and lists
	Cf. AS401 Serial directories
409	International serial publications
	Including the collections of extracts from the transactions of several learned societies
	For nonserial collections see AC1+
	Burma. Myanmar
428	General works
429	Learned periodicals
430.A-Z	Individual societies and institutions. By city, A-Z
	Subarrange individual societies or institutions by Table A4
	For learned periodicals of a society or institution see AS429
441-452	China (Table A18)
455	Taiwan (Table A19)
(457)	Hong Kong
	see AS441+
461-472	India (Table A18)
474	Nepal (Table A19)
475	Sri Lanka. Ceylon (Table A19)
	Southeast Asia
480	General
(481)	Bangladesh
	see AS567
482	Cambodia (Table A19)
484	Laos (Table A19)
486	Malaysia (Table A19)
492	Singapore (Table A19)
494	Thailand (Table A19)
496	Vietnam (Table A19)
511-522	Indonesia (Table A18)
	Philippines
539	General works
539.5	Learned periodicals
540.A-Z	Individual societies and institutions. By city, A-Z
	Subarrange individual societies or institutions by Table A4
	For learned periodicals of a society or institution see AS539.5
541-552	Japan (Table A18)
559	Korea (Table A19)
567	Bangladesh (Table A19)
569	Pakistan (Table A19)
571	Iran (Table A19)

	By region or country
	Asia -- Continued
	Central Asia
580	Kazakhstan (Table A19)
581	Kyrgyzstan (Table A19)
582	Tajikistan (Table A19)
584	Uzbekistan (Table A19)
	Near East. Southwestern Asia
587	Arabia (Table A19)
588	Armenia (Table A19)
588.2	Azerbaijan (Table A19)
588.5	Georgia (Republic) (Table A19)
589	Iraq (Table A19)
591	Israel. Palestine (Table A19)
593	Jordan (Table A19)
595	Lebanon (Table A19)
597	Syria (Table A19)
	Turkey see AS348
599	Other (not A-Z)
599.4	Arab countries
599.5	Islamic countries
	Africa
600	General
	Former British possessions
	General
601	Periodicals devoted to the interests of learned societies in general
(602)	Yearbooks see AS601
	International associations, congresses, conferences, etc.
602.5	General works
	Individual associations, etc.
604	General works
604.Z9A-.Z9Z	Projects for intellectual cooperation. By author, A-Z
605	Historical and descriptive literature. Handbooks For yearbooks see AS601 For directories and lists issued periodically see AS608
606	Organization of societies, conventions, congresses, etc. Including committees
607	Anniversary planning
608	Directories and lists Cf. AS601 Serial directories

	By region or country
	Africa
	Former British possessions
	General -- Continued
609	International serial publications
	Including the collections of extracts from the transactions of several learned societies
	For nonserial collections see AC1+
	Union of South Africa
611	General
613	Cape of Good Hope
615	Natal
617	Orange Free State. Orange River Colony
619	South African Republic. Transvaal
620	Botswana (Table A19)
620.4	Lesotho (Table A19)
621	Malawi (Table A19)
622	Zimbabwe. Rhodesia, Southern (Table A19)
623	Zambia (Table A19)
624	Kenya (Table A19)
625	Uganda (Table A19)
629	Somalia (Table A19)
631	Ghana (Table A19)
633	Nigeria (Table A19)
	Former French possessions
	General
641	Periodicals devoted to the interests of learned societies in general
(642)	Yearbooks
	see AS641
	International associations, congresses, conferences, etc.
642.5	General works
	Individual associations, etc.
644	General works
644.Z9A-.Z9Z	Projects for intellectual cooperation. By author, A-Z
645	Historical and descriptive literature. Handbooks
	For yearbooks see AS641
	For directories and lists issued periodically see AS648
646	Organization of societies, conventions, congresses, etc.
	Including committees
647	Anniversary planning
648	Directories and lists
	Cf. AS641 Serial directories

AS

By region or country
Africa
Former French possessions
General -- Continued

649	International serial publications

	Including the collections of extracts from the transactions
	        of several learned societies
	    For nonserial collections see AC1+

651	Algeria (Table A19)
653	Tunis (Table A19)
657	Madagascar (Table A19)
658	Senegal (Table A19)
659.A-Z	Other, A-Z
	Subarrange individual countries by Table A17
	Former German possessions
	General
661	Periodicals devoted to the interests of learned societies in general
(662)	Yearbooks
	see AS661
	International associations, congresses, conferences, etc.
662.5	General
	Individual associations, etc.
664	General works
664.Z9A-.Z9Z	Projects for intellectual cooperation. By author, A-Z
665	Historical and descriptive literature. Handbooks

	For yearbooks see AS661
	    For directories and lists issued periodically see
	        AS668

666	Organization of societies, conventions, congresses, etc.
	Including committees
667	Anniversary planning
668	Directories and lists
	Cf. AS661 Serial directories
669	International serial publications

	Including the collections of extracts from the transactions
	        of several learned societies
	    For nonserial collections see AC1+

671	Tanzania (Table A19)
673	Cameroon (Table A19)
675	Namibia. Southwest Africa (Table A19)
679.A-Z	Other, A-Z
681	Former Italian possessions
685	Zaire. Congo (Democratic Republic). Belgian Congo (Table A19)

	By region or country
	Africa -- Continued
	Portuguese Africa
687	Angola (Table A19)
688	Mozambique (Table A19)
689	Spanish Africa
	Other states
691	Ethiopia (Table A19)
693	Egypt (Table A19)
695	Liberia (Table A19)
697	Morocco (Table A19)
699.A-Z	Other, A-Z
	Subarrange individual countries by Table A19a
	e.g.
699.S8	Sudan (Table A19a)
	Oceania
	General
701	Periodicals devoted to the interests of learned societies in general
(702)	Yearbooks
	see AS701
	International associations, congresses, conferences, etc.
702.5	General works
	Individual associations, etc.
704	General works
704.Z9A-.Z9Z	Projects for intellectual cooperation. By author, A-Z
705	Historical and descriptive literature. Handbooks
	For yearbooks see AS701
	For directories and lists issued periodically see AS708
706	Organization of societies, conventions, congresses, etc.
	Including committees
707	Anniversary planning
708	Directories and lists
	Cf. AS701 serial directories
709	International serial publications
	Including the collections of extracts from the transactions of several learned societies
	For nonserial collections see AC1+
711-722	Australia (Table A18)
	New Zealand
748	General works
749	Learned periodicals
750.A-Z	Individual societies and institutions. By city, A-Z
	Subarrange individual societies or institutions by Table A4
	For learned periodicals of a society or institution see AS749

	By region or country
	Oceania -- Continued
	Pacific islands
761	Guam (Table A19)
(763)	Hawaii
	see AS28.H3
767	Samoan Islands (Table A19)
771	Fiji (Table A19)
773	Papua New Guinea (Table A19)
775	Tonga (Friendly Islands) (Table A19)
781	New Caledonia (Table A19)
785.A-Z	Other, A-Z
	Subarrange individual countries by Table A19a
	Other associations, "funds," foundations, and institutions
	Class here associations, etc. not provided for elsewhere in AS32+ and not provided for with special subjects in other classes
911.A2	General works
911.A4-Z	Special associations, "Funds," Foundations, etc., A-Z
	Subarrange each assocation by Table A4
	Awards, prizes, etc.
	For awards or prizes relating to a special subject or issued by a particular organization, see the subject or organization
935	General works
940	Directories. Lists
945.A-Z	By region or country, A-Z

	Yearbooks. Almanacs. Directories
	Annuals: Keepsakes, etc.
	American
10	History and criticism
11	Through 1860
12	1861-
	English language annuals other than American
13.A2	History and criticism
13.A3-Z	Through 1860
14	1861-
	French
15.A2	History and criticism
15.A3-Z	Through 1860
16	1861-
	German
17.A2	History and criticism
17.A3-Z	Through 1860
18	1861-
19.A-Z	Other languages, A-Z
	Christmas and other special numbers of magazines, etc.
	Prefer Subclass AP
21	American
23	English language magazines other than American
25	French
27	German
29.A-Z	Other languages, A-Z
	Almanacs
	Class here general, popular almanacs and yearbooks only
	For scientific and technical almanacs, see special subjects in Subclass AS, and Classes B-Z
	History of almanacs
30	General
	United States
31.A1	English
31.A5-Z	Other languages
32	Canadian
33	Other English language almanacs
34	French
35	German
36	Italian
37	Scandinavian
38	Spanish
39.A-Z	Other languages, A-Z
40	Universal collections
(41-49)	Early almanacs
	see AY51+ and Table A5, subdivisions 0-1, under each country
	By region or country

AY

	Almanacs
	By region or country -- Continued
	United States
	Early through 1799
	Prefer F1+
	Collections. By date of first volume
51.A001-.A699	Through 1699
51.B00-.B99	1700-1799
53	Serial. By title or editor
57	Other (Occasional issues). By date
59	Yearbooks (without almanacs)
	1800-
61	Collections. By title or editor
64	General. By title or editor
67.A-Z	Newspaper. By name of place, A-Z
	Subarrange by title
68	Magazine and literary almanacs
(70)	Institutions. Societies
	see subclasses AM, AS, and classes B-Z
71	Other recent English almanacs. By date
	Almanacs in foreign languages or for foreign nationalities
72.A-Z	French. By city of imprint, A-Z
	Subarrange by title
73.A-Z	German. By city of imprint, A-Z
	Subarrange by title
	Cf. AY78.S9 Swiss almanacs
74	Italian
	Arrange by title
75	Scandinavian (Danish, Norwegian, Swedish)
	Arrange by title
76	Slavic (Czech, Bulgarian, Polish, Russian)
	Arrange by title
77	Spanish
	Arrange by title
78.A-Z	Other languages or nationalities, A-Z
	Subarrange each language by title
78.C4	Cherokee
78.D8	Dutch
78.E6	Estonian
78.F5	Finnish
78.G8	Greek
78.H8	Hungarian
78.I8	Irish. Irish-American
78.J5	Jewish
78.L38	Latvian
78.L5	Lithuanian
78.R7	Romanian

	Almanacs
	By region or country
	United States
	Almanacs in foreign languages or for foreign nationalities
	Other languages or nationalities, A-Z -- Continued
78.S9	Swiss
78.T38	Tamil
78.T52	Tibetan
78.Y58	Yiddish
81.A-Z	By subject, A-Z
	Class here popular almanacs only
	For scientific and technical almanacs, see special subjects in Subclass AS, Classes B-Z
	For special nationalities see AY72+
	Agriculture see S414
(81.A8)	Astrological
	see BF1651
81.C7	Comic
81.C75	Commercial
81.D7	Dreams
81.E4	Educational
81.F3	Farmers'
81.F5	Financial
81.F6	Firemen's
81.G8	Grocers'
81.H7	Household
81.I6	Insurance
81.J6	Journalists'
81.J8	Juvenile
	Ladies' almanacs see AY81.H7
81.M3	Mathematical
81.M4	Medical
(81.M5)	Meteorological
	see QC999
81.M8	Musical
81.P3	Patent medicine
81.P7	Political
	Religious almanacs
81.R5A-.R5Z	By title (except Catholic almanacs), A-Z
81.R6A-.R6Z	Catholic almanacs. By title (except titles beginning with "Saint"), A-Z
81.R7A-.R7Z	Titles beginning with "Saint." By name of Saint
	e.g.
81.R7A6	Anthony
	Sports see GV158.A+
81.T3	Temperance
81.W3	Water-cure

AY

	Almanacs
	By region or country
	United States
	By subject, A-Z -- Continued
(81.W4)	Weather
	see QC999
	Women's almanacs see AY81.H7
81.W7	Workingmen's
(101-346)	Local. By state
	see F1+
(381.A-Z)	Confederate States almanacs
	see F206+
	Other regions or countries
	British America
	Canada
	Early through 1799
410	Collections. By date of first volume
411.A-.Z699	Serial. By title or editor, A-Z
411.Z7	Other. By original date of publication
412	Yearbooks (without almanacs)
	Prefer classification by subject in Classes B-Z
	1800-
413	Collections
414.A-Z	General. By title or editor, A-Z
415.A-Z	Newspaper, etc. By name of place, A-Z
	Subarrange by title
	Other
416.A3-.Z3	Literary and magazine almanacs, etc. By title or editor, A-Z
416.Z5	Miscellaneous. Occasional issues. By date
417	French. General almanacs
418	Other than English or French
419.A-Z	By subject, A-Z
419.C75	Commercial
419.F3	Farmers'
419.R6	Religious
(420)	Local
	see F1035.8+
425.A-Z	Other, A-Z
	e.g.
425.B4	Bermudas
	British Guiana see AY660+
425.J4	Jamaica
	Latin America
430-439	Mexico (Table A5)
	Central America
440-449	Costa Rica (Table A5)

Almanacs
  By region or country
    Other regions or countries
      Latin America
        Central America -- Continued

450-459	Guatemala (Table A5)
460-469	Honduras (Table A5)
470-479	Nicaragua (Table A5)
480-489	El Salvador (Table A5)
490-499	Panama (Table A5)

West Indies
  Bermuda see AY425.B4

510-519	Cuba (Table A5)
530-539	Haiti (Table A5)

Jamaica see AY425.J4

550-559	Dominican Republic (Table A5)
570-579	Puerto Rico (Table A5)
581.A-Z	Other, A-Z

South America

600-609	Argentina (Table A5)
610-619	Bolivia (Table A5)
620-629	Brazil (Table A5)
630-639	Chile (Table A5)
640-649	Colombia (Table A5)
650-659	Ecuador (Table A5)
660-669	Guyana (Table A5)
670-679	Suriname (Table A5)
680-689	French Guiana (Table A5)
690-699	Paraguay (Table A5)
700-709	Peru (Table A5)
710-719	Uruguay (Table A5)
720-729	Venezuela (Table A5)

Europe
  Great Britain

750-759	General (Table A5)
760-769	Scotland (Table A5)
770-779	Ireland (Table A5)
780-789	Wales (Table A5)

Austria
  Early through 1799

800	Collections. By date of first volume
801.A-.Z699	Serial. By title or editor, A-Z
801.Z7	Other. By original date of publication
802	Yearbooks (without almanacs)

Prefer classification by subject in Classes B-Z

1800-

803	Collections

	Almanacs
	By region or country
	Other regions or countries
	Europe
	Austria
	1800- -- Continued
804.A-Z	General. By title or editor, A-Z
805.A-Z	Newspaper, etc. By name of place, A-Z
	Subarrange by title
	Other
806.A3-.Z3	Literary and magazine almanacs, etc. By title or editor, A-Z
806.Z5	Miscellaneous. Occasional issues. By date
807.A-Z	Almanacs in foreign languages. By language, A-Z
808.A-Z	Special. By subject, A-Z
	Prefer classification by subject in Classes B-Z, e.g. BF1651 Prophetic almanacs
808.C7	Comic
808.H7	Household
808.J5	Jewish
	Labor union see AY808.T7
808.P7	Political
808.R6	Religious
808.T7	Trade union. Labor union
(809)	By state
	see DB101+
(810)	By city
	see DB841+
811-819	Hungary (Table A5)
820-829	Czechoslovakia (Table A5)
	Finland see AY990+
830-839	France (Table A5)
850-860	Germany
	Early through 1799
850	Collections. By date of first volume
851.A-.Z699	Serial. By title or editor, A-Z
851.Z7	Other. By original date of publication
852	Yearbooks (without almanacs)
	Prefer classification by subject in Classes B-Z
	1800-
853	Collections
854.A-Z	General. By title or editor, A-Z
855.A-Z	Newspaper, etc. By name of place, A-Z
	Subarrange by title
	Other
856.A3-.Z3	Literary and magazine almanacs, etc. By title or editor, A-Z

Almanacs
By region or country
Other regions or countries
Europe
Germany
1800-
Other -- Continued

856.Z5	Miscellaneous. Occasional issues. By date
857.A-Z	Almanacs in foreign languages. By language, A-Z
858.A-Z	Special. By subject, A-Z
	Prefer classification by subject in Classes B-Z, e.g.
	BF1651 Prophetic almanacs
858.C7	Comic
858.E4	Educational
858.F3	Farmers'
858.H7	Household
858.J4	Jewish
858.J8	Juvenile
858.P7	Political
	Religious
858.R5A-.R5Z	By title (except Catholic almanacs), A-Z
858.R6A-.R6Z	Catholic almanacs. By title, A-Z
(859)	By state
	see DD801.A+
(860)	By city
	see DD851+
870-879	Greece (Table A5)
	Including Greeks in Asia and Africa
890-899	Italy (Table A5)
	Netherlands
900-909	General (Table A5)
910-919	Belgium (Table A5)
920-929	Holland (Table A5)
930-939	Poland (Table A5)
940-949	Russia (Table A5)
949.5	Belarus
	Scandinavia
950-959	Denmark (Table A5)
960	Iceland
970-979	Norway (Table A5)
980-989	Sweden (Table A5)
990-999	Finland (Table A5)
1000-1009	Spain (Table A5)
1010-1019	Portugal (Table A5)
	Switzerland
	Early through 1799
1020	Collections. By date of first volume

AY

Almanacs
  By region or country
    Other regions or countries
      Europe
        Switzerland
          Early through 1799 -- Continued

1021.A-.Z699	Serial. By title or editor, A-Z
1021.Z7	Other. By original date of publication
1022	Yearbooks (without almanacs)
	Prefer classification by subject in Classes B-Z
	1800-
1023	Collections
1024.A-Z	General. By title or editor, A-Z
1025.A-Z	Newspaper, etc. By name of place, A-Z
	Subarrange by title
	Other
1026.A3-.Z3	Literary and magazine almanacs, etc. By title or editor, A-Z
1026.Z5	Miscellaneous. Occasional issues. By date
1027.A-Z	Almanacs in foreign languages. By language, A-Z
1028.A-Z	Special. By subject, A-Z
	Prefer classification by subject in Classes B-Z, e.g. BF1651 Prophetic almanacs
(1029.A-Z)	By canton
	see DQ301+
(1030)	By city
	see DQ851.A2+
	Balkan States
1038.A2	General works
1038.A3-Z	By region or country, A-Z
	e.g.
1038.A4	Albania
1038.B67	Bosnia and Hercegovina
1038.B8	Bulgaria
1038.C87	Croatia
	Hercegovina see AY1038.B67
1038.R8	Romania
1038.S59	Slovenia
	Turkey see AY1187
1038.Y6	Yugoslavia
1039.A-Z	Other European, A-Z
	e.g.
1039.E8	Estonia
1039.L8	Luxemburg
1039.M2	Malta
	Asia
1050-1059	India (Table A5)

	Almanacs
	By region or country
	Other regions or countries
	Asia -- Continued
	Far East
1120-1129	Philippines (Table A5)
1140-1149	China (Table A5)
1150-1159	Japan (Table A5)
1165.A-Z	Other, A-Z
	e.g.
1165.I5	Indonesia
	Southwestern Asia
1183	Israel
1185	Iran
1187	Turkey
1188.A-Z	Other Asian, A-Z
	Africa
	British Africa
1200-1209	South Africa (Table A5)
1231-1232	Kenya (Table A6)
1235-1236	Nigeria (Table A6)
1241-1242	Rhodesia (Table A6)
	French Africa
1251-1252	Algeria (Table A6)
1255-1256	Tunis (Table A6)
1501-1502	Zaire. Congo (Democratic Republic). Belgian Congo (Table A6)
1551-1552	Egypt (Table A6)
1555-1556	Ethiopia (Table A6)
1561-1562	Liberia (Table A6)
1571-1572	Morocco (Table A6)
1599.A-Z	Other, A-Z
	Australia
1600-1609	General (Table A5)
(1611-1612)	New South Wales
	see DU150+
(1615-1616)	Queensland
	see DU250+
(1621-1622)	South Australia
	see DU300+
(1625-1626)	Tasmania
	see DU182+
(1631-1632)	Victoria
	see DU200+
(1635-1636)	Western Australia
	see DU350+
1651-1652	New Zealand (Table A6)

AY

	Almanacs
	By region or country
	Other regions or countries -- Continued
	Pacific Islands
1671-1672	Guam (Table A6)
(1675-1676)	Hawaii
	see DU620+
1681-1682	Samoa (Table A6)
1730.A-Z	Other, A-Z
2001	Directories. General works on the compilation of directories, etc.
	Class directories by subject in classes B - Z

                History of scholarship and learning. The humanities
                   This subclass is not to be confused with Subclass CB, History of
                      civilization and culture, which includes, but which is broader in
                      concept than, scholarship and learning
                Periodicals, societies, congresses see AS1+
                Collections see AC1+

(20-48)	General works
	see AZ200+
	Philosophy. Theory
101	General works
103	Value, aims, influences etc. Addresses, essays, lectures.
	Pamphlets
	Methods. Organization
105	General works
106	Miscellany and curiosa
(107)	Classification
	see BD240+
	Cf. Z696+ Classification (Bibliography)
108	Symbols and their use
	Cf. P99+ Signs and symbols in communication
	Relation to special sciences
111	General works
(121)	Philosophy
	see B53+
(126)	Religion
	see BL1+
(131)	Social and political institutions
	see H61; JA71
(136)	Law
	see class K
(141)	Education
	see LB51+
(151)	Art
	see N72
(161)	Literature
	see P33+ P61+ PN45+
(171)	Science
	see Q175
	Medicine see R702
(181)	Technical sciences, inventions
	see T14
	Study and teaching
182	General works
183.A-Z	By region or country, A-Z
	Subarrange each by author
	Research

	Research -- Continued
186	General works
187	Directories
188.A-Z	By region or country, A-Z
	Subarrange each by author
	Evaluation
191	General works
192	Directories
193.A-Z	By region or country, A-Z
	Subarrange each by author
195	Electronic information resources
	Includingcomputer network resources, the Internet, digital libraries, etc.
	History
	General works
	Early works through 1800
200	Latin
201	English
202	French
203	German
204	Italian
208.A-Z	Other, A-Z
	19th century
211	English
212	French
213	German
214	Italian
218.A-Z	Other, A-Z
	20th century
221	English
222	French
223	German
224	Italian
228.A-Z	Other, A-Z
	21st century
231	English
232	French
233	German
234	Italian
238.A-Z	Other, A-Z
	By period
301	Antiquity
311	Ancient Oriental
	Including Assyro-Babylonian, Egyptian, etc.
321	Middle Ages
331	Renaissance

	History
	By period -- Continued
	Modern
341	General works
346	16th and 17th centuries
351	18th century
356	19th century
361	20th century
362	21st century
	By region or country
	America
501	General
	North America
502	General works
	United States
503	General
504	Colonial period
505	19th and 20th centuries
507	General special. Relation, aspects, etc.
508	Addresses, essays, lectures. Pamphlets
509	New England
510	South
511	West
513.A-Z	By region or state, A-Z
	e.g.
513.H3	Hawaii
(514.A-Z)	By city, A-Z
	see class F
515-516	Canada (Table A11)
	Latin America
517-518	Mexico (Table A11)
	Central America
519	General
521-522	Belize (Table A11)
523-524	Costa Rica (Table A11)
525-526	Guatemala (Table A11)
527-528	Honduras (Table A11)
529-530	Nicaragua (Table A11)
531-532	El Salvador (Table A11)
533-534	Panama (Table A11)
	West Indies
535	General
537-538	Bahamas (Table A11)
539-540	Cuba (Table A11)
541-542	Haiti (Table A11)
543-544	Jamaica (Table A11)

	By region or country
	America
	Latin America
	West Indies -- Continued
545-546	Puerto Rico (Table A11)
547.A-Z	Other, A-Z
	South America
548	Collections
549	General works. History
550	Addresses, essays, lectures. Pamphlets
551-554	Argentina (Table A9)
556-557	Bolivia (Table A11)
560-563	Brazil (Table A9)
565-568	Chile (Table A9)
570-571	Colombia (Table A11)
572-573	Ecuador (Table A11)
574-575	Guyana (British Guiana) (Table A11)
576-577	Suriname (Dutch Guiana) (Table A11)
578-579	French Guiana (Table A11)
581-582	Paraguay (Table A11)
583-584	Peru (Table A11)
585-586	Uruguay (Table A11)
587-588	Venezuela (Table A11)
	Europe
600-607	General (Table A7a)
	Great Britain
610-617	General works (Table A7a)
620-623	England - Local (Table A9)
625-628	Scotland (Table A9)
630-633	Ireland (Table A9)
635-638	Wales (Table A9)
638.5	Central Europe (Table A12)
640-649	Austria (Table A7)
649.5	Czechoslovakia (Table A12)
650-659	France (Table A7)
660-669	Germany (Table A7)
670-673	Greece (Table A9)
675-676	Hungary (Table A11)
680-689	Italy (Table A7)
690-699	Netherlands. Holland (Table A7)
700-709	Belgium. Flanders (Table A7)
709.5	Eastern Europe. Slavic countries (Table A12)
710-713	Russia (Table A9)
713.3	Belarus (Table A12)
713.4	Moldova (Table A12)
713.5	Ukraine (Table A12)

	By region or country
	Europe -- Continued
714-715	Poland (Table A11)
716-717	Finland (Table A11)
	Scandinavia
720-727	General (Table A7a)
728	Denmark (Table A12)
729	Iceland (Table A12)
730	Norway (Table A12)
731	Sweden (Table A12)
	Slavic countries see AZ709.5
740-749	Spain (Table A7)
750-753	Portugal (Table A9)
755-758	Switzerland (Table A9)
760	Turkey (Table A12)
	Balkan States
761	General (Table A12)
762	Bulgaria (Table A12)
763	Albania (Table A12)
764	Romania (Table A12)
764.5	Slovenia (Table A12)
765	Yugoslavia. Serbia (Table A12)
	Asia. The Orient
770	General (Table A12)
	Near East. Southwestern Asia
771	General works (Table A12)
772	Armenia (Table A12)
773	Iran (Table A12)
	Turkey in Asia see AZ760
775	Central Asia (Table A12)
	Southern Asia
776	General (Table A12)
777	India (Table A12)
778	Ceylon (Table A12)
	Southeast Asia
779	General (Table A12)
781	Vietnam (Table A12)
782	Thailand (Table A12)
783	Malaysia (Table A12)
785	Indonesia (Table A12)
787	Philippines (Table A12)
	Eastern Asia
789	General (Table A12)
791	China (Table A12)
793	Japan (Table A12)
794	Korea (Table A12)

AZ

	By region or country
	Asia. The Orient -- Continued
795	Siberia (Table A12)
	Africa
800-807	General (Table A7a)
810-819	Egypt (Table A7)
821.A-Z	Other divisions, A-Z
	Australia
850	General
851-854	New South Wales (Table A9)
861-864	Queensland (Table A9)
866-869	South Australia (Table A9)
871-874	Tasmania (Table A9)
876-879	Victoria (Table A9)
881	West Australia (Table A12)
891	New Zealand (Table A12)
	Pacific islands
901	General
908.A-Z	Individual islands or groups of islands, A-Z
	e.g.
	Hawaii see AZ513.H3
(950)	Biography
	see CT and the subdivision "Biography" under classes and subjects in classes B - Z
(990)	Anecdotes of scholars, professors, etc.
	see PN6231.S3, PN6259+
999	Popular errors and delusions

The Library of Congress no longer uses Table A1 except for
museums already so established in AM in its shelflist

0	Collections, etc.
1	Acts of incorporation, statutes, bylaws, rules, and regulations. By date
2	Administration. List of officers, etc.
2.5	Examinations
3	Annual reports
4	Other general serials not limited to a subject field: periodicals, collections, memoirs, etc.
4.5	Other minor official reports. By date
5	Guidebooks, catalogs. By date
5.2	Special minor exhibits. By date
6	History
6.5	Descriptive works (Official). By date
7	General works (Nonofficial)
9	Miscellaneous printed matter, circulars, announcements. By date

TABLES

The Library of Congress no longer uses Table A2 except for societies and institutions already so established in AS in its shelflist

The captions and order of publications are merely suggestive and may have been modified to meet the requirements of special cases. The numbers are also suggestive and may have been used as given or modified as needed.

1	Proceedings and transactions
2	Collections: Bulletins, contributions, memoirs, etc.
3	Periodicals. Yearbooks
4	Annual reports
4.5	Other reports (nonserial)
5	Congresses and conferences. Expositions
6	Constitution and bylaws
7	Directories. Lists of members
8	History of biography. Handbooks

For handbooks issued annually, see subdivisions 2, 3, 4, or 7, as the case may be

9	Addresses, essays, lectures
9.9	Miscellaneous printed matter: Announcements, programs, etc.

The Library of Congress no longer uses Table A3 except for societies and institutions already so established in AS in its shelflist. An obsolete variant of this table used 3 successive Cutter numbers.

.x12-.x19	Serial publications
.x2-.x29	Official monographs
.x3	Nonofficial publications

Use this table for any society newly established in Class A. In the AS subclass, when the form caption indicates that the society should be Cuttered by place, Cutter for the place, use a digit to represent the society, and double Cutter using this table.

	Official serials. By title
.xA1-.xA29	Titles beginning A-H
.xA3-.xA39	Titles beginning I-Q
.xA4-.xA49	Titles beginning R-Z
.xA5-.xA7	Official monographs. By title
.xA8-.xZ	Nonofficial publications

	Early through 1799
0	Collections. By date of first volume
1.A-.Z699	Serial. By title or editor, A-Z
1.Z7	Other. By original date of publication
2	Yearbooks (without almanacs)
	Prefer classification by subject in Classes B-Z
	1800-
3	Collections
4.A-Z	General. By title or editor, A-Z
5.A-Z	Newspaper, etc. By name of place, A-Z
	Subarrange by title
	Other
6.A3-.Z3	Literary and magazine almanacs, etc. By title or editor, A-Z
6.Z5	Miscellaneous. Occasional issues. By date
7.A-Z	Almanacs in foreign languages. By language, A-Z
8.A-Z	Special. By subject, A-Z
	Prefer classification by subject in Classes B-Z, e.g. BF1651
	Prophetic almanacs
	Agriculture
	see S414
(8.A8)	Astrological
	see BF1651
8.C7	Comic
8.C75	Commercial
8.D7	Dreams
8.E4	Educational
8.F3	Farmers'
8.F5	Financial
8.F6	Firemen's
8.G8	Grocers'
8.H7	Household
8.I6	Insurance
8.J6	Journalists'
8.J8	Juvenile
	Ladies almanacs see A5 8.H7
8.M3	Mathematical
8.M4	Medical
(8.M5)	Meteorological
	see QC999
8.M8	Musical
8.P3	Patent medicine
8.P7	Political
	Religious almanacs
8.R5A-.R5Z	By title (except Catholic almanacs), A-Z
8.R6A-.R6Z	Catholic almanacs. By title (except titles beginning with "Saint"), A-Z

TABLES

	1800-
	Special. By subject, A-Z
	Religious almanacs -- Continued
8.R7A-.R7Z	Titles beginning with "Saint". By name of Saint
	e.g.
8.R7A6	Saint Anthony
	Sports
	see GV185
8.T3	Temperance
8.W3	Water-cure
(8.W4)	Weather
	see QC999
	Women's almanacs see A5 8.H7
8.W7	Workingmen's
(9)	Local
	see classes D-F

1	Collections and general
2.A-Z	Local
	see class D

0	Collections
	General works. History
1	General works
2	Early. Origins
3	Middle Ages
4	Modern
6	General special. Relations, aspects, etc.
7	Addresses, essays, lectures. Pamphlets
8.A-Z	States, regions, provinces, etc., A-Z
(9)	Cities
	see subclasses DA-DU and Classes E-F

Apply this table to regions that are larger than a single country
0   Collections
               General works. History
1   General works
2   Early. Origins
3   Middle Ages
4   Modern
6   General special. Relations, aspects, etc.
7   Addresses, essays, lectures. Pamphlets

1	Collections
2	General works. History
3	Addresses, essays, lectures. Pamphlets
4.A-Z	States, regions, provinces, etc., A-Z
(5)	Cities
	see subclasses DA-DU and Classes E-F

1	Collections
2	General works. History
3	Addresses, essays, lectures. Pamphlets
4.A-Z	States, regions, provinces, etc., A-Z

1.A1-.A3	Collections
1.A5-.Z3	General works. History
1.Z5	Addresses, essays, lectures. Pamphlets
2.A-Z	States, regions, provinces, etc., A-Z
(3)	Cities
	see subclasses DA-DU and Classes E-F

1.A1-.A3	Collections
1.A5-.Z3	General works. History
1.Z5	Addresses, essays, lectures. Pamphlets
2.A-Z	States, regions, provinces, etc., A-Z

TABLES

0.A1-.A2	Collections
0.A5-.Z3	General works. History
0.Z5	Addresses, essays, lectures. Pamphlets
0.Z7A-.Z7Z	States, regions, provinces, etc., A-Z
(0.Z8)	Cities
	see subclasses DA-DU and Classes E-F

1   Several authors
2   Individual authors

1	General works
2.A-Z	States, provinces, etc., A-Z
3.A-Z	Cities, towns, etc., A-Z

1.A1	Periodicals. Societies
1.A2	General works
1.A3-Z	Provinces, etc., A-Z
2.A-Z	Cities, towns, etc., A-Z

.A2	General works
.A3A-.A3Z	States, provinces, etc., A-Z
.A4-.Z	Cities, towns, etc., A-Z

.x	General works
.x2A-.x2Z	States, provinces, etc., A-Z
.x3A-.x3Z	Cities, towns, etc., A-Z

TABLES

1	Periodicals and documents about the learned societies, institutions, etc., of the country
(2)	Yearbooks, etc. see A18 1
3.A-Z	Individual conferences, congresses, etc., A-Z
4	Conferences, congresses, etc. Class conferences, congresses, etc., of individual societies, etc. with the society
5	Historical and descriptive literature. Handbooks
6.A-Z	History. By state, region, province, etc., A-Z
7.A-Z	History. By city, A-Z
8	Directories and lists
11	Learned periodicals
12.A-Z	Individual societies and institutions. By city, A-Z Subarrange each by tables A2, A3, or A4 For learned periodicals of a society or institution see A18 11

	General works
.A1	Periodicals
	Including learned periodicals
(.A2)	Yearbooks
	see A19 .A1
.A3	Congresses
	History. Handbooks
.A5	General
.A6A-.A6Z	Local, A-Z
.A7	Directories. Lists
.A8-.Z	Individual societies and institutions. By city, A-Z
	Subarrange each by Table A4
	For learned periodicals of a society or institution see A19 .A1

	General works
.xA1	Periodicals
	Including learned periodicals
(.xA2)	Yearbooks
	see A19a .xA1
.xA3	Congresses
	History. Handbooks
.xA5	General
.xA6-.xA69	Local, A-Z
.xA7	Directories. Lists
.xA8-.xZ	Individual societies and institutions. By city, A-Z
	For learned periodicals of a society or institution see A19a
	.xA1

INDEX

A

Academies (General): AS1+
African periodicals (General)
  in
    English: AP9
    French: AP27
    German: AP35
Afrikaans periodicals (General): AP18
Agricultural almanacs
  Popular farmer's almanacs: AY81.F3
Albanian periodicals (General):
  AP95.A3
Almanacs (General): AY30+
American periodicals (General)
  in
    Armenian: AP95.A8
    Czech: AP53
    Danish: AP43
    English: AP2.A2+
    French: AP21.A2+
    German: AP31
    Hungarian: AP83
    Italian: AP38
    Japanese: AP95.J25
    Norwegian: AP46
    Polish: AP55
    Portuguese: AP66
    Russian: AP51
    Spanish: AP62+
    Swedish: AP49
American periodicals, Humorous:
  AP101.A+
American periodicals, Juvenile:
  AP201.A+
Amharic periodicals (General):
  AP95.A4
Annamese periodicals (General):
  AP95.V5
Annuals (General): AY10+
Arabic periodicals (General): AP95.A6
Archives, Museum: AM158
Armenian periodicals (General):
  AP95.A7+
Asian periodicals (General)
  in
    English: AP8

Asian periodicals (General)
  in
    French: AP26
    German: AP34
Assamese periodicals (General):
  AP95.A85
Associations, International (General):
  AS2.5+
Australian periodicals (General)
  in
    English: AP7
    French: AP28
Authorship (Encyclopedias): AE1.5
Azerbaijani periodicals (General):
  AP95.A92

B

Baluchi periodicals (General): AP95.B3
Belarusian periodicals (General):
  AP58.W5
Belgian periodicals (General): AP22
Bengali periodicals (General): AP95.B4
Bisaya periodicals (General): AP95.B55
Blacks, Periodicals for (General)
  Juvenile periodicals: AP230
Books, Reference: AG1+
British periodicals (General): AP2.A2+,
  AP3+
Bulgarian periodicals (General):
  AP58.B8
Burmese periodicals (General):
  AP95.B9

C

Canadian periodicals (General)
  in
    English: AP5
    French: AP21.A2+
Canarese periodicals (General):
  AP95.K3
Catalan periodicals (General): AP95.C3
Catholic International Scientific
  Congress: AS4.C3
Celtic periodicals (General): AP73+
Children's museums: AM8

German periodicals (General)
  Juvenile periodicals: AP205+
Gorkhali periodicals (General):
  AP95.N4
Greek (Modern) periodicals (General):
  AP85
Greenlandic periodicals (General):
  AP95.E37
Grocers' almanacs: AY81.G8
Gujarati periodicals (General): AP95.G8

H

Hawaiian periodicals (General):
  AP95.H2
Hebrew periodicals (General): AP91
  Juvenile periodicals: AP221
Hindi periodicals (General): AP95.H5
Household almanacs: AY81.H7
Humanities (General): AZ19.2+
Humorous periodicals (General):
  AP101+
Hungarian periodicals (General):
  AP82+

I

Icelandic periodicals (General): AP41
Ilocano periodicals (General): AP95.I46
Inaugural dissertations: AC801+
Indexes (General): AI1+
Indexes, Newspaper: AI21.A+
Indonesian periodicals (General):
  AP95.I5
Insurance almanacs: AY81.I6
International associations, congresses,
  etc.: AS2.5+
International periodicals (General): AP1
Internet
  Academies and learned societies:
    AS8.5
  Humanities: AZ195
  Museums: AM215
Irish (Celtic) periodicals (General):
  AP73
Italian periodicals (General): AP37+
  Humorous periodicals: AP107

Italian periodicals (General)
  Juvenile periodicals: AP207

J

Japanese periodicals (General):
  AP95.J2+
Javanese periodicals (General):
  AP95.J3
Jewish readers
  Collections for: AC200
  General periodicals for: AP91+
  Juvenile periodicals for: AP221+
Journalists' almanacs: AY81.J6
Juvenile almanacs: AY81.J8
Juvenile reference books: AG5+,
  AG103+

K

Kanarese periodicals (General):
  AP95.K3
Kannada periodicals (General):
  AP95.K3
Karelian periodicals: AP95.K33
Kazakh periodicals (General):
  AP95.K35
Khas periodicals (General): AP95.N4
Kirundi periodicals (General): AP95.R8
Konkani periodicals (General):
  AP95.K57
Korean periodicals (General): AP95.K6

L

Ladies' almanacs: AY81.H7
Latin (Medieval and modern)
  periodicals: AP95.L35
Latvian periodicals (General): AP95.L4
Learned societies: AS1+
Lithuanian periodicals (General):
  AP95.L5
Lost and found objects
  Musuems: AM501.L67

M

Macedonian periodicals (General):
AP58.M25
Magyar periodicals (General): AP82+
Malabar periodicals (General):
AP95.M25
Malagasy periodicals (General):
AP95.M2
Malay periodicals (General): AP95.M24
Malayalam periodicals (General):
AP95.M25
Marathi periodicals (General): AP95.M3
Mathematical almanacs: AY81.M3
Medical almanacs: AY81.M4
Monographs (General collections):
AC1+
Mundari periodicals (General):
AP95.M84
Murathee periodicals (General):
AP95.M3
Museology: AM111+
Museum archives: AM158
Museum information, Communication of:
AM125
Museums: AM1+
Museums and people with disabilities:
AM160
Museums, Children's (General): AM8
Musical almanacs: AY81.M8

N

National Endowment for the Humanities:
AS35
Nepali periodicals (General): AP95.N4
New Zealand periodicals (General)
in
English: AP7.5
French: AP28.5
German: AP36.5
Newari periodicals (General):
AP95.N43
Newspapers: AN
Individual newspapers
Indexes: AI21.A+

Norwegian periodicals (General):
AP45+
Notes and queries (Reference books):
AG305+

O

Objects, Lost and found
Museums: AM501.L67
Oddities
Reference books: AG240+
Oriya periodicals (General): AP95.O7

P

Pacific islands periodicals (General)
in
English: AP7.7
French: AP28.7
German: AP36.7
Pamphlet collections (General):
AC901+
Panjabi periodicals (General):
AP95.P25
Parbate periodicals (General): AP95.N4
Patent medicine almanacs: AY81.P3
People with disabilities and museums:
AM160
Periodicals (General): AP1+
By learned societies: AS1+
Persian periodicals (General): AP95.P3
Pictorial works (Reference books):
AG250
Polish periodicals (General): AP54+
Political almanacs: AY81.P7
Polyglot periodicals (General): AP1
Popular almanacs: AY81.A+
Popular errors, delusions, and
superstitions: AZ999
Portuguese periodicals (General):
AP65+
Humorous periodicals: AP111
Juvenile periodicals: AP211
Private collections: AM200+
Program dissertations: AC801+
Provençal periodicals (General):
AP95.P7

Q

Queries: AG305+
Questions and answers (Reference
  books): AG195+
Quiz books: AG195+

R

Raeto-Romance periodicals (General):
  AP95.R3
Rajasthani periodicals (General):
  AP95.R35
Reference books (General): AG1+
Religious almanacs: AY81.R5+
Romanian periodicals (General): AP86
Romansh periodicals (General):
  AP95.R3
Rundi periodicals (General): AP95.R8
Russian periodicals (General): AP50+
Ruthenian periodicals (General):
  AP58.U5

S

Sanskrit periodicals (General): AP95.S3
Scandinavian periodicals (General):
  AP40+
  Humorous periodicals: AP109
  Juvenile periodicals: AP209
Scholarship and learning, History of:
  AZ19.2+
Scientific almanacs: AS1+
Scottish (Celtic) periodicals (General):
  AP75
Scrapbooks: AC999
Security measures
  Museums: AM148
Serbian periodicals (General): AP56
Sindhi periodicals (General): AP95.S5
Sinhalese periodicals (General):
  AP95.S54
Slavic periodicals (General): AP50+
Slovak periodicals (General): AP58.S53
Slovenian periodicals (General):
  AP58.S55
Societies, Learned: AS1+

Sorbian periodicals (General): AP58.S6
Soyot periodicals (General): AP95.S6
Spanish periodicals (General): AP60+
  Humorous periodicals: AP111
  Juvenile periodicals: AP211
Sundanese periodicals (General):
  AP95.S8
Swahili periodicals (General): AP95.S9
Swedish periodicals (General): AP48+
Swiss periodicals (General)
  in
    French: AP24
    German: AP32
    Italian: AP39
    Raeto-Romance: AP95.R3

T

Tagalog periodicals (General):
  AP95.T27
Tajik periodicals (General): AP95.T28
Tamil periodicals (General): AP95.T3
Tatar periodicals (General): AP95.T34
Technical almanacs: AS1+
Telugu periodicals (General): AP95.T4
Temperance almanacs: AY81.T3
Turkish periodicals (General): AP95.T8
Turkmen periodicals (General):
  AP95.T83

U

Ukrainian periodicals (General):
  AP58.U5
UNESCO: AS4.U8+
United Nations Educational, Scientific
  and Cultural Organization: AS4.U8+
Urdu periodicals (General): AP95.U7
Uriya periodicals (General): AP95.O7

V

Vietnamese periodicals (General):
  AP95.V5
Views (Pictorial reference books):
  AG250

INDEX

W

Water-cure almanacs: AY81.W3
Welsh (Celtic) periodicals (General):
    AP77
Wendic periodicals (General): AP58.S6
White Russian periodicals (General):
    AP58.W5
Wikipedia: AE100
Women's almanacs: AY81.H7
Women's reference books: AG5+,
    AG103+
Wonders
    Reference books: AG240+
Workingmen's almanacs: AY81.W7

Y

Yearbooks (General): AY10+
Yiddish periodicals (General): AP91
    Juvenile periodicals: AP221

GPO U.S. GOVERNMENT PRINTING OFFICE: 2012–378–911/40021